People of the Bible

The Bible through stories and pictures

Jesus the Healer

First Steck-Vaughn Edition 1992

Copyright © in this format Belitha Press Ltd, 1986

Text copyright © Catherine Storr 1986

Illustrations copyright © Chris Molan 1986

Art Director: Treld Bicknell

ISBN 0-8172-2041-0

Conceived, designed and produced by Belitha Press Ltd.,
2 Beresford Terrace, London N5 2DH

Library of Congress Cataloging in Publication Data

Storr, Catherine.
  Jesus the healer.

  (People of the Bible)
  Summary: Retells the life of Jesus Christ as he
teaches, preaches, and performs miracles.
    1. Jesus Christ—Biography—Juvenile literature.
2. Christian biography—Palestine—Juvenile literature.
[1. Jesus Christ—Biography. 2. Bible stories—N.T.]
I. Title. II. Series.
BT302.S879 1985   232.9′01 [B]   85-12282

First published in Great Britain in paperback 1986
by Methuen Children's Books Ltd
11 New Fetter Lane, London EC4P 4EE

  3 4 5 6 7 8 9   98 97 96 95 94 93

Jesus the Healer

Retold by Catherine Storr
Pictures by Chris Molan

RAINTREE
STECK-VAUGHN
L I B R A R Y
The Steck-Vaughn Company

After Jesus had called his disciples
together they all went about in Galilee,
teaching and healing the people.

One Sabbath day in Capernaum they were in the synagogue, and there they saw a man possessed by a devil. The devil in him called out, "Let us alone, Jesus of Nazareth. Have you come to destroy us? I know you, you are the Holy One of God."

Jesus said to the devil, "Be quiet and come out of this man." The devil tormented the man terribly, but then it came out and the man was healed and in his right mind again.

The people were amazed. They said,
"What sort of teaching is this? What power
has this man to cast out devils?" Everyone
in Galilee heard of what had happened.

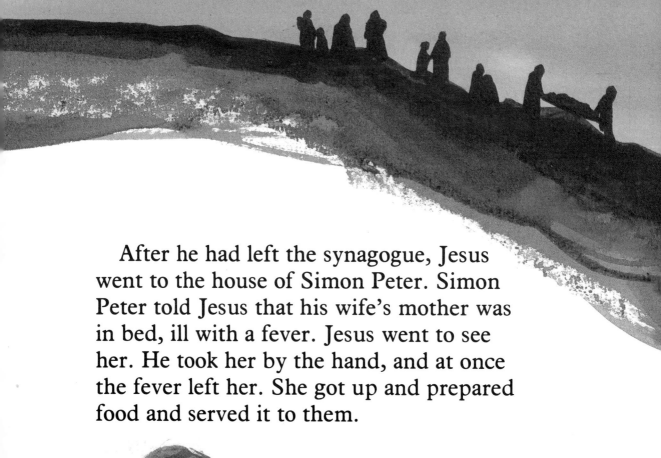

After he had left the synagogue, Jesus went to the house of Simon Peter. Simon Peter told Jesus that his wife's mother was in bed, ill with a fever. Jesus went to see her. He took her by the hand, and at once the fever left her. She got up and prepared food and served it to them.

That evening when the sun was set, a great many people were brought to the door and Jesus healed them.

The next morning he got up before the sun had risen and went to a solitary place to pray.

Simon Peter and the other disciples followed him and said, "Everyone is looking for you."

Jesus said, "We will go into the next towns to heal and preach there, for that is what I have come for."

While he was teaching, a man who was ill with leprosy came up to Jesus and said, "Lord, will you cure me?"

Most people were afraid to touch a leper in case they might catch the disease. But Jesus took the man by the hand and said, "I will help you. You shall become clean."

At once the leprosy disappeared and the man was healed. Jesus said to him, "Don't tell anyone except your priest about this and make an offering to God in thanksgiving."

On another Sabbath day, when Jesus was teaching in the synagogue, the Scribes and the Pharisees were waiting and watching. They wanted to get Jesus into trouble by saying that he was breaking the law by working on the Sabbath. They watched as Jesus came near to a man who had a withered hand.

Jesus knew what they were thinking. He asked them, "Is it against the law to do good on the Sabbath? Or to do evil? Should we save life or destroy it?"

He said to the man, "Stretch out your hand." As the man did this, his hand was healed.

Then the Scribes and Pharisees were furious and hated Jesus still more. They consulted with each other about how they could destroy him.

Jesus and his disciples left the towns and went to the sea, but they were followed by great crowds from Galilee and from Judea and from Jerusalem and from Tyre and Sidon because they had heard what great things he had done.

The crowds were pressing very close.
Jesus said to his disciples, "Get a small ship
to wait off shore for us."

After he had healed many ill people and
cast out many devils, he got into the ship
and sat in it, a little way out into the sea,
and taught the people from there.

That evening, Jesus said to his disciples,
"Let us sail over to the other side of the
sea." They set sail with other little ships.

But a great storm arose, and the waves
beat over the side of the ship so that it
became full of water. The disciples were
terrified. They saw that Jesus was asleep at
the back of the ship.

They woke him and said, "Master, don't you care if we are all drowned?"

Jesus rose up and rebuked the wind and the sea, saying, "Peace. Be still!" Then the wind dropped and the sea became calm.

Jesus said to the disciples, "Why were you so frightened? Why don't you have more faith?"

On the other side of the sea, in the land of the Gadarenes, there lived a man who had been mad for a long time. He lived among tombs, where he ran about naked, crying out loudly and cutting himself with sharp stones. He was so wild that no one could bind him with fetters or chains.

When he saw Jesus, he fell down and cried, "Jesus, Son of God, do not torment me!"

Jesus said, "You are possessed by devils," and he commanded the devils to leave the man.

The devils obeyed Jesus. They fled into a herd of swine which were feeding on the side of the mountain. When the swine felt the devils come into them, they ran down the side of the mountain and fell into the sea and were drowned.

But the man was healed. He sat at the feet of Jesus, wearing clothes, and was sensible once more.

Jesus went on into Capernaum, and there an important Roman citizen, a Centurion, said to him, "One of my servants is ill. He is paralyzed and can't move."

Jesus said, "I will come to your house to heal him."

But the Centurion said, "I am not worthy that you should come to my house. In the army, we give orders. If I say to a man,

'Go!', he goes, and if I say 'Come!', he comes, and what I tell my servant to do, he does. If you will just say the word, my servant will be healed."

Jesus turned to the people around him and said, "This man has more faith in me than I have found in all Israel." To the Centurion he said, "Because you have believed in me, your servant is already healed."

One day, Jesus took three of his disciples, Peter, James, and John, up onto a high mountain, away from everyone else. There, the three disciples saw Jesus transfigured. His clothes became shining and whiter than snow, and the disciples saw Elijah and Moses talking to him. Peter said, "Master, it is good for us to be here."

Then a cloud overshadowed the figures and a voice said, "This is my beloved Son. You should listen to him."

When the cloud disappeared, they saw
only Jesus standing there. As they came
down from the mountain, Jesus said,
"Don't tell anyone about this until the Son
of Man has risen from the dead."

Jesus was in the house of Simon the leper. As he sat at the table, a woman of the city came in, carrying an alabaster box of spikenard, a very precious ointment. She kneeled at Jesus' feet and washed them with her tears. Then she dried them with her hair and anointed them with the ointment.

The disciples said, "What a waste! The woman could have sold that ointment and given the money to the poor."

Jesus said, "Let her alone. She has brought this ointment to be ready for my burying. The poor are always with you, but I shall not always be with you. This woman has many sins, but she has also loved much, and for that, her sins are all forgiven her."

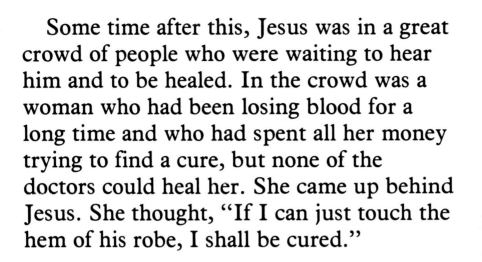

Some time after this, Jesus was in a great crowd of people who were waiting to hear him and to be healed. In the crowd was a woman who had been losing blood for a long time and who had spent all her money trying to find a cure, but none of the doctors could heal her. She came up behind Jesus. She thought, "If I can just touch the hem of his robe, I shall be cured."

As she touched the robe, the blood
stopped flowing. Jesus said, "Someone has
touched me! I felt the power go out of me."

He turned around and saw the woman,
who trembled and fell down before him.
She told him that she had touched his robe
so that she might be healed.

Jesus said, "Be comforted, my daughter.
Your faith has made you whole."

Jesus knew that at the Feast of the Passover he must go to Jerusalem where his enemies would capture him and kill him. He told his disciples, but they did not understand. They traveled toward Jericho, and on the road they passed a blind man, sitting by the roadside. His name was Bartimaeus. He asked, "Who are these people whose footsteps I hear going past?"

The people said, "Jesus of Nazareth is going along this road."

Bartimaeus called out, "Jesus, son of David, have mercy on me!"

The people scolded him, "Be quiet!"

But he cried out again, "Have mercy on me!"

Jesus stopped and said, "Bring him here." Then he asked him, "What do you want me to do for you?"

The blind man said, "Lord, I want to recover my sight."

Jesus said, "You shall recover your sight. Your faith has saved you."

As Jesus went through Jericho, he was surrounded by an enormous crowd. The chief of the tax-gatherers, a very rich man called Zacchaeus, wanted to see Jesus, but as he was a small man, he could not see over the heads of the crowds. So he ran in front of the people and climbed up into a tree to get a better view. When Jesus went past the tree, he looked up and saw Zacchaeus.

He said, "Zacchaeus, make haste and come down, for today I shall stay in your house."

Zacchaeus quickly climbed down and joyfully took Jesus to his house. Some of the people complained and said, "Jesus is staying with a man who is a sinner."

But Jesus said to Zacchaeus, "Today, salvation has come to your house, for you are a son of Abraham. The Son of Man is come to save those who were lost."

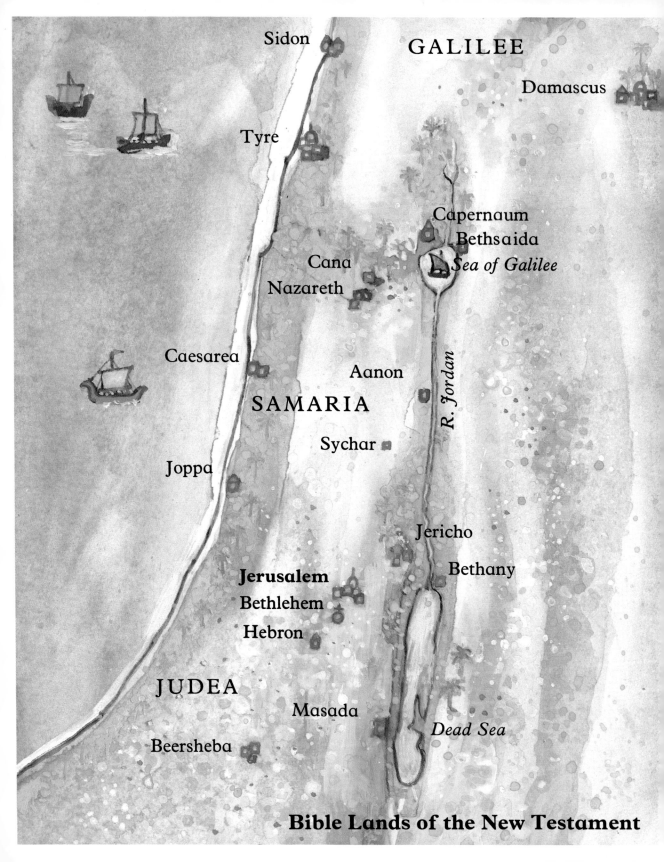

Sidon

GALILEE

Damascus

Tyre

Capernaum
Bethsaida
Sea of Galilee

Cana
Nazareth

Caesarea

Aanon

SAMARIA

Sychar

R. Jordan

Joppa

Jericho
Bethany

Jerusalem
Bethlehem
Hebron

JUDEA

Masada

Dead Sea

Beersheba

Bible Lands of the New Testament